Stars in the Garden
FRESH FLOWERS IN APPLIQUÉ

PIECE O' CAKE DESIGNS, INC.
Becky Goldsmith and Linda Jenkins

Martingale
& COMPANY
Bothell, Washington

Credits

Technical Editors	Janet White, Ursula Reikes
Design and Production Manager	Cheryl Stevenson
Cover Designer	Jim Gerlitz
Text Designer	Marijane E. Figg
Copy Editor	Liz McGehee
Illustrator	Laurel Strand
Photographer	Brent Kane

MISSION STATEMENT

We are dedicated to providing quality products and service by working together to inspire creativity and to enrich the lives we touch.

Stars in the Garden: Fresh Flowers in Appliqué
© 1998 by Becky Goldsmith and Linda Jenkins
Martingale & Company, PO Box 118
Bothell, WA 98041-0118 USA

Printed in the United States of America
03 02 01 00 99 98   6 5 4 3 2 1

Acknowledgments

No one makes it alone, least of all us! First, we must thank our husbands, Steve and Paul. Steve is our first editor, making sure that what we have written makes sense even to a non-quilter. Paul is our shipping manager who keeps things running smoothly. We love you both and appreciate your support.

It is not possible to get through this life without good friends. It certainly would not be any fun! Barbara Nimon and Linda Muirhead are always there to get the job done. We appreciate their friendship and upbeat attitudes. Many thanks go to Karen Stone and Muriel McIver for their encouragement and friendship.

We thank our editors, Janet White and Ursula Reikes, for their help and encouragement. It is a pleasure to work with them both.

Library of Congress Cataloging-in-Publication Data

Goldsmith, Becky,
    Stars in the garden : Fresh flowers in appliqué / Piece
O'Cake Designs, Inc., Becky Goldsmith, and Linda Jenkins.
      p. cm.
    ISBN 1-56477-223-3
    1. Appliqué—Patterns. 2. Patchwork—patterns. 3. Patchwork
quilts. 4. Decoration and ornament—Plant forms. I. Jenkins,
    Linda, II. Piece O'Cake Designs. III. Title.
TT779.G63 1998
746.46'041—dc21
                                      98-10349
                                        CIP

Table of Contents

Stars in the Garden

70" x 90"

Read all directions before beginning.

Introduction

Whether the flower garden is real or imagined, every one is full of stars. There are twelve different flowers in our garden. In each block, the flowers dance around a central star. These designs are reminiscent of the graceful blocks that our grandmothers made, but are as fresh as flowers picked from today's garden.

Coloring Your Quilt

We choose the background fabric for our quilts first. This may seem like an easy and obvious task, but we give it serious thought. We want a background that shows off the appliqué to its best advantage. In times past, the usual choice was off-white muslin. Today we have so many more options. The background fabric sets the mood for the whole quilt, and the possibilities range from dramatic darks to tranquil pastels.

There is no one, perfect color for the background of any quilt. You can choose a light, medium, or dark value in any color. (Value is where, in the range from lightest to darkest, a color lies.) You can piece together many fabrics, as we did for the larger blocks, or you can use one fabric. Your choices are unlimited. Choose a color that you want to work with, the one that makes you the happiest, and you are on your way to coloring the rest of your quilt.

Keep in mind, though, that the background is not the focal point of the quilt. A pieced background should provide a subtle texture for the appliqué to shine against. To piece the background as we did, choose fabrics that are very similar in value and scale (the size of the design). *Remember that the background should remain in the background.*

The visual appeal of your quilt depends on getting the right mix of values in the fabrics you choose. Light, medium, and dark values are all represented in the gray scale below. See the difference between the squares that are farthest apart? Squares that are next to each other are more difficult to tell apart. Contrast is the difference in value between two or more colors. The higher the contrast between fabrics that are next to each other in your quilt, the more those fabrics stand out. When we want to emphasize a particular part of a design, using high-contrast fabrics is one way we do it. If we want subtle shading in an area of a design, we use fabrics with lower contrast. View your fabrics with a red value finder if you are having trouble determining their values.

⭐ Note from Linda: You need a big stash of fabric! Buy lots of fat quarters, fewer big chunks of fabric. The more variety in your stash, the better.

Gather many fabrics in the color and value you have chosen for your pieced background. Stack the fabrics so that you can see a small part of each one. Stand back from your stack and remove any fabric that is wildly different from the rest.

Special instructions for the miniature blocks:

For the miniature Stars in the Garden quilt, Linda chose a background that was not too busy. She chose fabrics that are solid or nearly solid. A busy background could easily overpower the appliqué at such a small scale.

If your appliqué fabrics are the same value as your background fabric, you won't be able to see the appliqué well, regardless of the colors you choose. If you use a light background, use medium to dark fabrics for the majority of the appliqué. If you choose a dark background, use medium to light values for the majority of the appliqué. A medium-value background is perhaps the most difficult to work on because you must choose carefully among light and dark values for your applique.

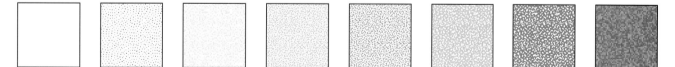

Areas of high contrast (light lights against strong darks) are visually striking. Areas of low contrast (light mediums against mediums) are more subtle. Including both high- and low-contrast areas in your appliqué makes it more interesting.

The scale of the print helps to determine the kind of visual texture that a fabric has. The sweeping brush strokes of a large floral print create a different visual texture than a well-defined stripe. Combining fabrics with different scale, value, and contrast in one flower creates a uniqueness that can make a block sing.

Now begin choosing your appliqué fabrics. You will need a wide range of greens for the leaves. Choose all kinds of greens: blue-greens, yellow-greens, olive greens, true greens. We mix these different greens in the same block. Find different values and scales of green prints. Begin stacking the appliqué fabrics as you did your background fabrics. Add brown and brown-green for stems to the stack. Last, but definitely not

least, choose flower fabrics. We used many colors in many values, and many scales of prints, plaids, stripes, and printed solids throughout the quilt. Add these flower fabrics to your stack of appliqué fabrics.

These appliqué projects require a large variety of small pieces of fabric. As you build your stacks, do not be too concerned about yardage amounts. Fat quarters (18" x 22") are usually sufficient for most projects. Have you ever been in the middle of a project and run short of a particularly important fabric? Don't worry. It has happened to us, and we have found that a sudden shortage can provide the opportunity for creative choices that make a quilt more interesting.

Now put the background stack next to the appliqué stack. At this point, it is not necessary to know where any one piece of fabric will be used. How do the appliqué fabrics look next to the background fabrics? Look at the stacks through a value finder. Do the two stacks run together, or is there contrast between the background stack and the appliqué stack? If any of the fabrics look out of place, remove them. Concentrate on building stacks of fabric that look fabulous together. There is no limit to the number of fabrics in either stack.

We enjoy the process of building fabric stacks for our quilts. Trust that if your stacks look good, your quilt will too. You can supplement your stacks with more fabric when necessary, but we find that it is easier and our quilts are more visually appealing when we gather the majority of the fabric for a quilt into harmonious stacks and work from them. Many times, we build stacks of fabric for fun before we know what quilt they will be used in!

Preparing Your Fabrics

Always prewash your fabrics. As a general rule, we prewash all of our fabrics before adding them to our stash. The laundering process washes out excess dye and factory sizing. Cotton fabric can shrink during the laundering process, and in hand appliqué, it is usually better that the fabric shrinks before being stitched. A prewashed fabric is also easier to needle-turn, and it feels better in your hand.

Once your fabric is washed, press it flat. Some fabrics, particularly woven stripe and plaid fabrics, handle better if you use a little spray sizing on the back as you iron. The sizing adds body to the fabric.

Fabric Requirements

for 70" x 90" Stars in the Garden

Block Backgrounds

There are sixteen pieces in each background block. The large blocks finish 20" square, but you will not piece together sixteen 5½" squares. The blocks will be handled a lot during the appliqué process, which tends to stretch and fray the outer edges. Appliqué can shrink the block slightly, so the outer pieces in each block are cut larger than the pieces in the center. Once the appliqué is complete, the outer edges of the blocks are trimmed to make the blocks the correct size for piecing.

Cut background pieces as follows from your stack of background fabrics. It is not necessary to plan where each and every piece goes; simply cut the squares and rectangles randomly from the stack of fabrics you have assembled.

> 48 squares, each 5½" x 5½"
> 48 squares, each 6½" x 6½"
> 96 rectangles, each 5½" x 6½"

Put the cut pieces up on a design wall as shown at right so that you can see how they look together. It is important to view the blocks on the wall at each stage of development. Looking at the pieces flat on the floor or on a table is just not as helpful. If you do not have a design wall, try to find a place to put up a piece of batting to use as a temporary design wall, perhaps pinned to a larger quilt already on a wall. Some background fabrics that looked good in your stack may

not look as good on the wall. It is easier to make changes before sewing the pieces together. Watch for fabrics that stick out like a sore thumb and replace them. View these pieces through a value finder if necessary.

When you are satisfied with the arrangement, piece your background blocks.

Place the blocks on your design wall in their proper positions.
Evaluate them. Sew them together into pairs.
Sew pairs together into four 4-patches.
Sew the 4-patches together into the whole block.

6½" square	5½" x 6½" rectangle	5½" x 6½" rectangle	6½" square
5½" x 6½" rectangle	5½" square	5½" square	5½" x 6½" rectangle
5½" x 6½" rectangle	5½" square	5½" square	5½" x 6½" rectangle
6½" square	5½" x 6½" rectangle	5½" x 6½" rectangle	6½" square

The miniature blocks finish 8" square. Cut the blocks 10" x 10". After the appliqué is complete, you will trim them to size. Press each block in half both vertically and horizontally to establish a center grid that you can use to align your overlay.

If you do not want to piece your background blocks, cut twelve 22" squares. You used to be able to count on a 44" width off the bolt, but that is seldom true today. More often, fabric shrinks to a 40" width after washing. If your prewashed fabric is 44" wide, you will need 3¾ yards. If it is less than 44" wide, you will need 7½ yards.

Sashing

These flower designs fill the blocks. In many instances, the edge of a flower petal ends ¼" from the seam line. For this reason, Becky chose sashing fabrics that were very similar to the fabrics in the block backgrounds. The sashing gives the designs room to "breathe" by visually separating them.

Do you want the viewer of your quilt to see the appliqué first? Look at many quilts and pay attention to what you see first. Go to page 24 and look at Stars in the Garden. Usually what your eye goes to first are the areas of strongest contrast: the lightest light against the darkest dark, or vice versa. Many quilts look better with sashing separating the blocks, but very often the sashing is in high contrast to the blocks. When this is true, what the viewer sees first is a grid created by the sashing.

You can make the sashing grid less obvious by choosing sashing fabrics similar in value to the block backgrounds. Subtle changes in value and scale in the sashing will usually set your blocks apart without allowing the sashing to dominate the quilt.

Once the appliqué is complete and the blocks are pressed and trimmed, we audition different sashing options with the blocks. Evaluate your blocks and sashing fabrics together on a design wall before you sew them together.

Cut sashing pieces as follows from fabric similar to your background fabrics.

15 horizontal sashing strips, each 1½" x 20½"
16 vertical sashing strips, each 1¾" x 20½"
20 corner rectangles, each 1½" x 1¾"

Outer Border

Cut the following squares for the outer border:
• 124 squares, each 3" x 3", of fabric similar to your background
• 496 squares, each 1¾" x 1¾", of fabric that is a *subtle to strong contrast* with your background.

Yes, that is a lot of squares, but you can cut them from strips!
• A 3" x 18" strip yields 6 squares, each 3" x 3".
• A 1¾" x 18" strip yields 10 squares, each 1¾" x 1¾".

Backing and Sleeve

You will need a total of 6 yards of fabric for the backing and sleeve.

Cording

Begin with a 29" square. Make a 2½"-wide continuous bias strip. Refer to cording instructions for further details.

Binding

Begin with a 34" square. Make a 3"-wide continuous bias strip for French binding.

Making Appliqué Templates

Each piece in each block is numbered. The numbers indicate the stitching sequence. The lowest number, #1, is stitched to the background first. Piece #2 is stitched next, and so on. Always number your templates on the right side, and keep the templates for each block together in a Ziploc bag.

We use three-ring binders with clear-plastic sleeve pages inside to keep all of the parts of a project together. Put the templates, the overlay, and any other materials relating to a block into its own sleeve in the binder. You will fill several sleeves for a large project. Label the spine of the binder with the title of the project, and the sleeves with the block name so you can find the project easily at a later date.

Templates the Easy Way

We like to photocopy the appliqué patterns and cut templates from the copies, covering them with Con-Tact paper to make them more durable. Photocopying is more accurate and less stressful than the traditional tracing method. Photocopied templates on Con-Tact paper are much easier to cut out than template plastic. They often fit together better and, because the pattern that you copied is numbered, so are your templates. However, if access to an accurate copy machine is difficult, or you just prefer to use template plastic, make your templates the traditional way.

Photocopy the quarter-block patterns on the pullout pattern, then cut out the appliqué shapes. Since many of the appliqué shapes overlap, you'll need multiple copies of each quarter block so you can get one of them from one sheet and the other from another sheet. Make five copies of each. Five is usually enough, but you won't need that many for every block, and you'll need more for others. Occasionally, you must draw in part of a template that is covered by another so that the template shape is complete.

Open a roll of clear Con-Tact paper and peel back 8" to 12" of the backing. Lay out the Con-Tact paper with its sticky side up. (A clear, self-adhesive laminating sheet works as well. Peel off the backing and stick it to your copies.) Lay one template copy sheet, with the drawn side down, on the sticky side of the Con-Tact paper. Cut out as many templates as possible from the first sheet. For those pieces that you were unable to cut from the first sheet, use the other copies. Remember to stick the drawn side of the paper to the sticky side of the Con-Tact paper. When cutting out your templates, cut down the center of the template outlines. Keep smooth edges smooth and points sharp. Many of the leaves have a reverse-appliquéd vein. For those leaves, make a template of the vein and another template of the whole leaf shape.

Note from Linda and Becky: Linda likes laminate sheets; Becky likes Con-Tact paper. Try both and pick the one you prefer.

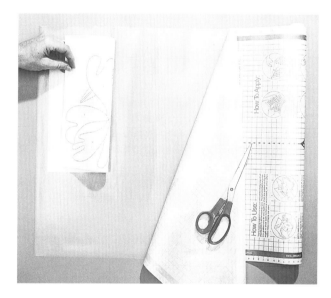

Using Appliqué Overlays As a Placement Guide

We use an overlay because it's accurate and portable. It's fast too! You don't have to go to a light box, and you don't draw on your background fabric.

An overlay is a drawing of the finished block on a clear piece of flexible plastic that you place over your background to help you position each piece. We use clear, 8- or 12-gauge upholstery vinyl to make our overlays. It comes on 60"-wide rolls. Check your local quilt shop or fabric store. If you have trouble locating upholstery vinyl, any clear, flexible, non-stretchy plastic can be used for an overlay.

Begin by cutting a 14" square of clear upholstery vinyl for each 20" block. (Cut an 8" square for each miniature block.) Each block in the Stars in the Garden quilt is made up of four identical quarters. Lay the plastic over the drawing of a quarter block and accurately trace the drawing with a permanent, fine-point marker. Include center dashed lines (see photo below). Leave room in one corner of the overlay to draw the entire star. Mark the numbering sequence on your overlay. There is a different center star in each block. Turn to the page with the star drawing and complete the center star. Include the seam lines of the star in your tracing. Keep the overlay for each block with the templates for that block.

Tip Upholstery vinyl comes with a tissue-paper liner sheet. Cut the vinyl without removing the tissue paper. Keep your overlay and its tissue paper together. If you lay the tissue paper on the right side of the vinyl before you fold it for travel or storage, it will prevent the marker lines from transferring to other parts of your overlay.

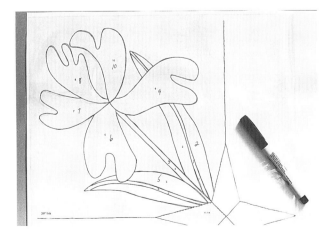

Make an overlay of the entire block for the miniature version of Stars in the Garden. Cut upholstery vinyl pieces 8" x 8" and be sure to mark the center of each side.

Designing a Block

Your templates and overlays are made. You have assembled beautiful stacks of fabrics for your quilt. Now it is time to design your first block. You can complete these blocks in any order, but we recommend beginning with a simple block, such as the "Iris."

You are going to hold an audition! Each fabric plays a special part in your block. You don't want to find out that you chose the wrong fabric after the block has been stitched, so audition each piece, choosing fabrics from your fabulous stacks.

⭐ ***Note from Becky:*** Don't be shy! Let even those colors you consider to be wallflowers audition for a part in your quilt.

There are no bad colors. Keep your mind open to the attributes of fabrics you wouldn't ordinarily use. If you are having trouble finding just the right color, try using one that you find unappealing—it may turn into one you can't do without.

Spread out the templates for the Iris block on your work surface. Find template #1 and choose a fabric from your stack for it. Refer to the photograph of the Iris block on page 30 for inspiration. Using a quilter's mechanical pencil or a sharpened chalk pencil, trace around the template onto the appliqué fabric, with both the template and the fabric right side up. Where possible, place templates on the diagonal grain of the fabric. It is easier to turn under a bias edge for the seam allowance than it is to turn under a straight-of-grain edge. Be sure to keep your drawn line close to the edges of the template so that you do not distort the size of the appliqué piece. A sandpaper board under the fabric keeps it from shifting as you trace the templates.

Cut out each appliqué piece, adding a seam allowance (see Tip on page 11). Where one appliqué piece lies under another, make the seam allowance a bit larger. Sometimes your appliqué can move and shrink a little, and it is better to have excess fabric to trim away than to not have enough. *Many of the stems and veins in the leaves are best appliquéd using a cutaway technique. Please read the instructions for this technique on pages 13–14 before cutting your fabric.*

Tip Use a larger seam allowance, ¼" or more, during the auditioning process. You will be handling these pieces quite a bit, and the extra fabric ensures that your seam allowance will not fray away. When you've made your final selections, trim the seam allowances to ³⁄₁₆".

Read the leaf instructions on pages 14–15. When choosing the fabrics for the leaves, keep the difference in value between the body of the leaf and the vein subtle. During the audition process, you may cut one or two leaf shapes with veins and place them on the block to give you an idea of how the leaves will look after stitching. You can then cut rectangles for the leaf bodies as described for cutaway appliqué.

Put your backgrounds up on your design wall. Begin the audition! After you have traced and cut piece #1, place it in position on the background. Choose a fabric for template #2 and cut it out. Lay piece #2 in position as well. Continue in this manner until all the appliqué pieces for this block are cut out and positioned on the background. Stand back and critique the block. Do any of the pieces look like they don't belong? Do some pieces fade into each other where they're not supposed to? You may need to audition other fabrics for these parts until you can say "Yes! Yes! You have the part!" Do not discard the "maybe" fabrics until you have made your final choice. ("We'll call you; don't call us.")

Note from Becky: I have learned not to rush through this phase of quilt design. I sometimes leave works in progress on the wall for days (weeks, months …) while working out the fabrics in a block.

The stars in the center of each block give you an opportunity to use plaids and stripes in a way that adds movement to the block. Using a fabric with a directional design will cause the star to twirl. Look at the block on page 20. Refer to "Preparing the Stars" on page 16 before cutting out the star fabrics.

You can work on one-quarter of the design at a time, or you can design the whole block at once. Just be sure to view the whole block on your design wall before you begin stitching. Use pins as necessary to keep the pieces in place, and be careful not to stretch your appliqué pieces. We chose not to repeat fabrics exactly in each quarter of the block. In most blocks, either parts of the leaves or parts of the flower (or both) contain different fabrics in each quarter.

We recommend that you design all of the blocks before you begin stitching. Designing all the blocks first allows you to get an idea of how they are going to look together, and it gives you the opportunity to make any changes that might be necessary. Though all are talented, not all players can be on the stage at the same time.

Once your blocks are designed, take them down and stack them for easy stitching. Stack the appliqué pieces for each block together. Find the highest-numbered piece and put it at the bottom of the stack. There are four appliqué pieces for each number. Stack all four together. You will stitch piece #1 first, so place it on the top of the stack last. Set the pieced star aside to keep it from stretching out of shape. Put your stacked appliqué pieces with their overlay and background into a Ziploc bag for easy storage until you are ready to stitch.

Let's go back to the Iris block. Position the overlay for the iris over one-quarter of the background, orienting the center dashed lines drawn on the overlay with the center seams in the background fabric. Following the stitching order as indicated on the drawing, slip piece #1 under the overlay and into position. Carefully pin it in place. Try using ½" sequin pins for this. Once you get used to this pin size, you will enjoy stitching without getting your thread hung up on pins. Stitch down piece #1. Do not stitch down any part of an appliqué piece that is covered by another appliqué piece.

Tip Finger-press all appliqué pieces before pinning them down. Make sure you turn under the drawn pencil or chalk line.

Working in a clockwise rotation, align your overlay over the next quarter of the block. Slip piece #1 in place in that quarter, pin, and stitch (see stitching instructions below). After you have stitched down four #1s, move back to the first quarter of the block and appliqué piece #2. As you become more practiced with this technique, you can position and pin more than one piece at a time.

Stitching the Appliqués

You are ready to begin stitching! You need thread to match all of the fabrics that you will be stitching down. We prefer a high-quality, 50-weight, 100% cotton thread. You also need appliqué needles. There are many needles on the market. Find the needle that suits you best. Try several. You may want a needle threader as well. Use a sharp pair of small scissors, such as Gingher's embroidery scissors. Don't underestimate the importance of good lighting and a comfortable chair. Your invisible stitches will be more invisible if you are comfortable and can easily see what you are doing. Unless you are working at a table, you will find a sandpaper lap board handy.

Use thread that matches the piece to be appliquéd. Thread the needle before cutting off the thread from the spool, then cut the thread about 18" long and knot the end that you just cut from the spool. Thread has a nap, and by knotting the cut end, you will ensure fewer kinks in your thread as you stitch.

> **Tip** Work with a thread about 18" long or shorter. A thread that is too long wears out and knots up. Reposition the eye of the needle on the length of thread often, so as not to wear weak spots in the thread.

Begin stitching away from a point or concave curve. Bring your needle up through the appliqué piece in a finger-pressed crease, then down through the background. The tail of your thread hides under the appliqué.

The invisible appliqué stitch is done one stitch at a time. Your needle remains on top of the work; do not "stick and stab" your stitches. The downward stitch goes into the background right next to the turned-under edge of the appliqué. The thread travels on the back and follows the outer edge of the appliqué. The upward stitch comes up into the appliqué piece, just catching its edge. Pull your thread tight enough to "sink" your stitches. Sinking the stitches pulls the appliqué firmly to the background and hides the stitches. Make each appliqué stitch approximately 1/16" long.

> **Tip** We generally recommend that you do not cut away background fabric from behind your appliqué for two reasons: the background will not fray out from behind your appliqué, and the quilt is more structurally sound if the background remains intact. However, these blocks feature a pieced star centered over a pieced background. We did cut away the very center pieced intersection of the background behind the star to minimize the thickness of the fabric in that spot.

Cutaway Appliqué Stems

We use the cutaway appliqué technique for many of the flower stems in this book. These long, skinny pieces are very hard to handle if they are cut out with a 3/16" seam. Leaving each stem as part of a larger piece of fabric keeps it from stretching out of shape and makes it easier to position as well. Some of the stems vary in width and look better when stitched using the cutaway technique. Others are of uniform thickness, allowing you to use a bias-stem technique (see page 14).

Laying the stem template on the diagonal grain of the fabric, cut a piece of fabric large enough for tracing the entire template. Leave ample room for the seam allowance. Lay the template, right side up, on the right side of your chosen fabric. Trace around it. Do not trim away the excess fabric. You can finger-press the edges of the stem while it is still part of the larger piece.

Using the overlay, position the stem fabric on the background. Pin it in place, being careful to keep the pins outside the drawn stem on the convex side. Stitch the inside (concave) curve of the stem down first. Begin by cutting away the fabric at the point where you want to begin stitching, leaving a scant 3/16"-wide seam allowance. Begin stitching, turning under the seam allowance as you go. Cut away more of the excess fabric as necessary. Clip curves only where necessary. Stitch down both sides of each stem.

Tip

The stars at the center of each block do not cover each stem in a block at the same place. It is a good idea to leave an inch or more at the base of each stem just in case the star doesn't cover as much of the stem as you think it will. It's better to have to cut off excess stem than to not have enough.

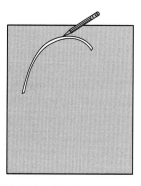

1. Fabric for the daisy stem with the stem template lying on the diagonal grain of the fabric. Trace the stem.

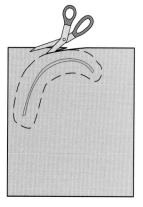

2. Cut the stem, with excess fabric, out of the bigger piece of stem fabric.

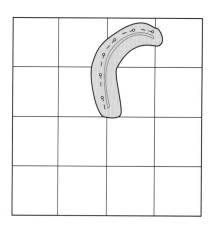

3. Use your overlay to position the stem on your background. Pin in place.

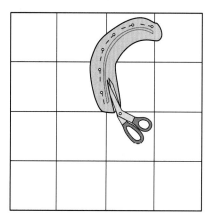

4. Begin cutting away the excess fabric, leaving a 3/16" seam allowance. Stitch the concave side of the stem first.

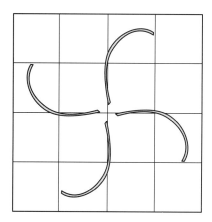

5. Continue in this manner until all four stems are stitched down.

The swirly flower center of the Pincushion Flower (page 32) is also stitched using the cutaway appliqué technique. Cut two squares of fabric for each flower, one for the top swirl and one for the bottom. Lay template #16 over the top-swirl fabric square and trace around it. Lay the top fabric square over the bottom-swirl fabric square, right sides up. Carefully cut down the center of the other part of the swirl, #15. The stitching line of #15 is curved. Clip the concave curves as necessary. Turn under the seam allowances and invisibly stitch the flower center. Trim, then stitch it in place on your block.

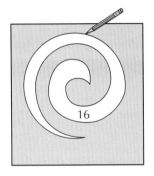

1. Trace around #16 onto the top swirl fabric.

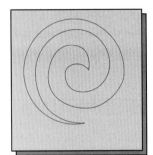

2. Lay the top-swirl fabric square over the bottom-swirl fabric square.

3. The dashed line is the cutting line. Cut, then stitch. Clip curves when necessary.

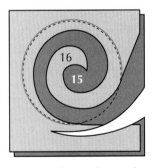

4. Cut out the #15/16 swirl 3/16" beyond the seam line (shown as dashed line). It is ready to stitch in place.

Bias Stems

You can make some of the flower stems using a bias-stem technique. This is another good way to handle a long, narrow, curvy appliqué piece. We use bias bars made from a heat-resistant plastic. You can also use metal Celtic bars.

To make bias stems, begin by cutting a 1½"-wide bias strip long enough for each stem. Lightly press each bias strip in half lengthwise, wrong sides together. Don't use steam and don't stretch the stem. Using the seam guide on your sewing machine to

make a ¼" seam, stitch the strip with the folded edge against the guide. Before you go too far, put the rounded end of your ¼" bias bar in the tube you just created, to make sure that it fits. You want to have the tiniest bit of play. Sew each bias strip in this manner.

Trim the seam allowance, leaving only enough to hold the stem together, about ⅛". Slide the ¼" bias bar into the stem, wiggle the seam to the back of the stem, and press the seam allowance to one side, so that both the seam allowance and the seam are hidden on the back of the bias stem. Press the stem with a hot iron while it is covering the bias bar and then again after you take out the bar. Position the stems on your block as directed above. Be sure to leave enough stem at either end to extend under both the flower and the center star.

★ **Note from Linda:** I save all of my bias-stem scraps. They come in handy for other projects.

Leaves

We used reverse appliqué to make the unusual veined leaves in this quilt. Begin by choosing the fabric for the body of a leaf and another fabric for the vein of the leaf. Lay the template for the body of the leaf, right side up, on the diagonal grain of the right side of the leaf fabric. Trace around the template. Next, position the vein template over the outline of the leaf drawn on the fabric. Trace the vein onto the leaf fabric. (You do not need to extend the part of the vein that becomes the stem.) Cut out the piece of fabric with the leaf and vein drawn on it, leaving 1" of fabric around it on all sides.

Pin the leaf fabric on top of the vein fabric, right sides up. Begin at the base of the leaf and cut down the center of the drawn vein, revealing the vein fabric below. Cut a little at a time. Turn the vein seam allowance under and stitch. Stop stitching at each end of the leaf and knot the thread. Begin stitching again on the opposite side of the vein, working your way along the center of the leaf until all of the vein is revealed.

★ **Note from Becky:** It happens to everyone sooner or later—you are working on a block and it just isn't looking right. Maybe your background is too busy, or the appliqué fabrics are running together. Stop! Put your block up on a wall and examine it. If it needs changing, change it now.

Lay the vein template over the stitched leaf. Gently move the fabric at the bottom of the leaf out of the way and trace the stem of the leaf onto the vein fabric. Now you can cut the leaf out of the larger piece of vein fabric. Be careful to leave a scant 3/16"-wide seam allowance on the sides of the stem and leave 1/2" at the base of the stem. Turn the fabric over and cut away the excess vein fabric. Leaving a 3/16"-wide seam allowance, trim away the outer edges of the leaf fabric. The leaf unit is ready to stitch in place on your block. Repeat this process for each leaf.

1. Place body of leaf template on leaf fabric. Trace around it.

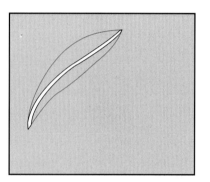

2. Lay the vein template over the leaf you have drawn on the fabric. Trace the vein.

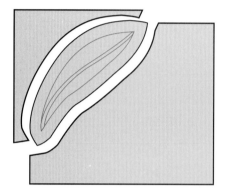

3. Cut out the drawn leaf and vein, leaving 1" excess fabric around it.

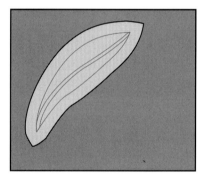

4. Place the leaf fabric over vein fabric.

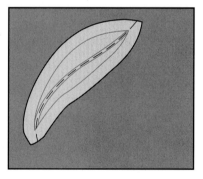

5. Cut down the dashed line at the center of the vein. Needleturn the raw edges under and stitch along the drawn line.

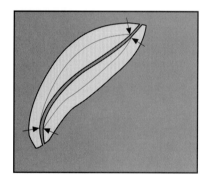

6. Stitch the vein. Stitch between the end points of the leaf, not into the seam allowance.

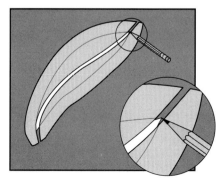

7. Lay the vein template over the stitched vein and trace both ends.

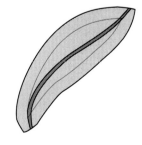

8. Cut the leaf away from the vein fabric.

9. Trim leaf, adding a 3/16" seam allowance. The leaf is ready to stitch in place.

Preparing the Stars

Directional fabrics, especially stripes and plaids, can make these stars truly shine in your garden. Stars made with directional fabrics have great visual movement. For best results when using these fabrics, make each diamond of the star identical. Choose one stripe to run the length of each diamond of the star and, if you are using a plaid fabric, align a crosswise stripe across the body of the diamond. Surprising and lovely patterns form in each star.

Piece your stars by hand or by machine. We chose to piece each star in the large quilt by machine. The miniature stars are pieced by hand.

Make a template for one diamond of each star. Choose a fabric for one of the stars. Position the diamond template, right side down, on the wrong side of the fabric and trace carefully around it. Make sure that the template is placed in exactly the same spot on the same stripe or design of the fabric each time you trace it. Cut out each diamond, adding a ⅜"-wide seam allowance.

The drawn line is the seam line. Pin the end points of the seam lines to make sure that they match exactly. Sew just inside the line. Once a seam is sewn, trim the seam allowance to ³⁄₁₆". Press seam allowances in the same direction around the star. When your star is complete, turn it over and place it, right side up, on your sandpaper board. Place the template over each diamond in the star and trace around its outer edges. Trim away the excess seam allowance. Your star is ready to appliqué in place.

There are stars with four, five, six, and eight points. Two of the eight-point stars are made of two four-point stars, one appliquéd on top of another. The star in the center of the Wild Honeysuckle block is not pieced at all, but is cut whole from one piece of fabric.

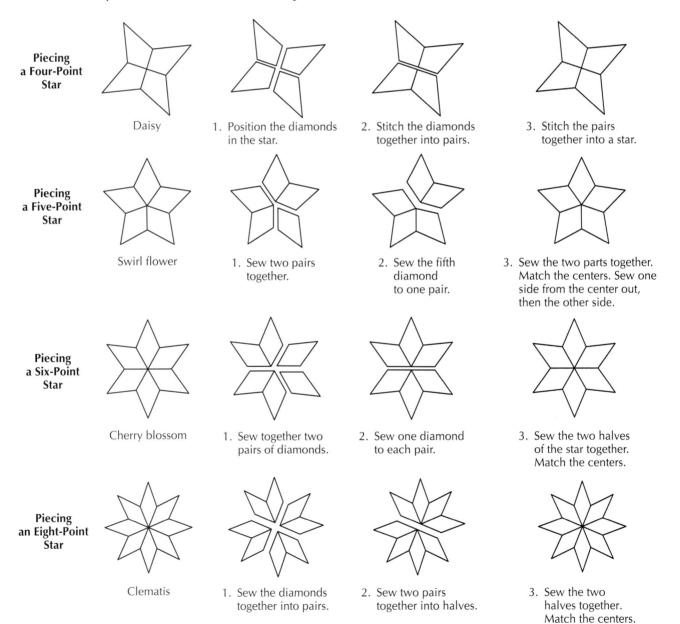

Piecing a Four-Point Star

Daisy

1. Position the diamonds in the star.

2. Stitch the diamonds together into pairs.

3. Stitch the pairs together into a star.

Piecing a Five-Point Star

Swirl flower

1. Sew two pairs together.

2. Sew the fifth diamond to one pair.

3. Sew the two parts together. Match the centers. Sew one side from the center out, then the other side.

Piecing a Six-Point Star

Cherry blossom

1. Sew together two pairs of diamonds.

2. Sew one diamond to each pair.

3. Sew the two halves of the star together. Match the centers.

Piecing an Eight-Point Star

Clematis

1. Sew the diamonds together into pairs.

2. Sew two pairs together into halves.

3. Sew the two halves together. Match the centers.

Gallery

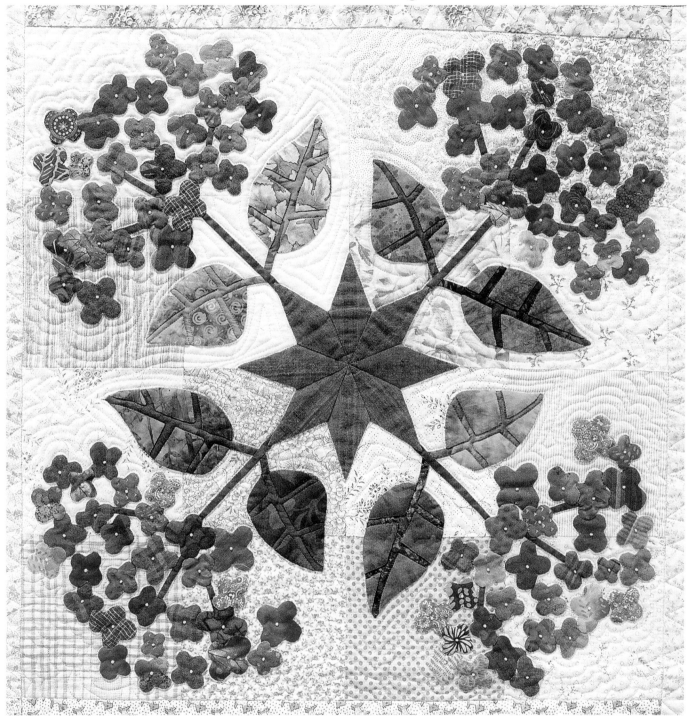

Hydrangea

Fanciful Fans

Star Flower

Cherry Swirl

Daisy

Dot's Delight

Peony

*Stars in the
Garden*
70" x 90"

Stars in My Little Garden
29½" x 29½"

Detail of "Stars in My Little Garden" blocks

Dogwood

Wild Honeysuckle

Iris

Clematis

Pincushion Flower

Piecing the stars for the miniature quilt is difficult. If you choose to piece them, follow the diagrams on page 16. Or, appliqué the diamonds in place on the block, working in a clockwise direction. An alternative is to treat each star as one unit, making one template for the whole star and cutting each star from one piece of fabric.

Trimming Your Blocks to Size

When your appliqué is complete, gently press the blocks, wrong side up. Remember the adage to measure twice, cut once. Carefully center and trim your blocks to 20½".

Adding the Sashing

Stitch the blocks, sashing strips, and corner rectangles together as shown. Use 1½"-wide strips for the horizontal sashing and 1¾"-wide strips for the vertical sashing. Remember to press the seam allowances toward the sashing strips at each step.

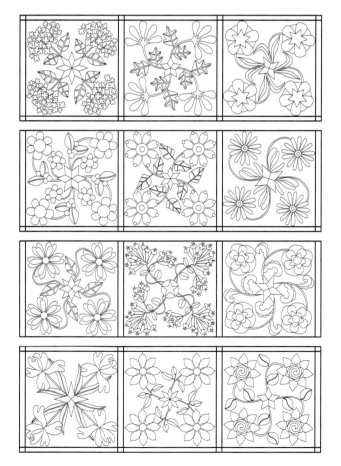

Stitching the Outer Border

Stars in the Garden has a pieced outer border composed of many fabrics. Because the border has so many pieces, even the slightest variation in your seam allowance can alter the size of your border strips, and then they won't fit. A ¼"-wide seam allowance can vary from sewing machine to sewing machine, so do not change sewing machines in the middle of this project. Sew several pieced squares, then stop and measure them to make sure that they really are 3" square. If not, adjust your seam allowance before continuing.

3" center sashing square

1¾" sashing corner

1. Sew one small square to two opposite corners of the 3" square. Trim away excess, leaving a ¼"-wide seam allowance.

2. Press the triangles to the outside.

3. Sew a small square to each of the other two corners. Trim excess seam allowance.

4. Press the triangles to the outside. This is one complete border block. It will finish to 2½".

Make 2 strips of 34 squares each for the side borders. Attach them to the body of the quilt first. Then attach 2 strips of 28 squares each for the top and bottom borders. Refer to the cording instructions and attach cording to the quilt top.

Finishing the Edges with Cording

Most quilts and wall hangings are finished with traditional bias or straight-grain binding. We like to use a corded edge for several reasons. Cording gives any quilt a tailored, finished look. Done well, it helps your quilt hang better because cording does not stretch, and it has body and strength that binding does not have. An added advantage of cording is that it is sewn on before you layer your quilt. As you quilt, the cording helps protect the outer edge of the quilt top from fraying and stretching.

Cording must be made from strips cut on the bias. Straight-grain strips don't cover the cord smoothly.

To add cording to your quilt top:

1. Measure the perimeter of your quilt top and add 15" to this measurement.
2. Make a 1½"-wide continuous bias strip from the 29" square of cording fabric. Cut a piece of cotton or polyester cording the same length.
3. Square up one end of the bias strip. Fold under 1½" of that end and press the fold. Beginning 1" from the fold, lay the cording down the center of the wrong side of the bias strip.

Leave 1" free of cord.

Lay cording down center.

4. Fold the bias fabric around the cording and stitch with a zipper foot and matching thread, butting the zipper foot against the covered cording. Once the entire length of the cording is encased in fabric, trim the seam allowance to ¼", leaving the first 1½" at the folded end untrimmed.

Match raw edges and stitch.

Leave 1½" of folded edge untrimmed.
Trim the remaining seam allowance to ¼".

5. Starting in an inconspicuous place on the lower right side of the quilt top, align the raw edges of the cording and the quilt top right sides together. Begin stitching 1½" from the folded end of the cording, using a ¼"-wide seam allowance.
6. The corners will be slightly curved, not pointed. Be sure to make the curve of each corner the same. As you stitch around each corner, gently push the cording into the corner. Do not pull on the cording or the quilt top as you sew.

Cording

Because the fabric is cut on the bias, the seam allowance stretches here.

> **Tip**
> If you are going to machine quilt, you can still attach the cording to the quilt top before adding the batting and backing. However, machine quilting draws up your quilt more than hand quilting does, so it is important to pull ever so gently on the cording as you attach it if you are machine quilting. It will draw up the outer edges of your top slightly, but the cording will fit after machine quilting. Consider practicing on scrap fabric before stitching the cording to your quilt.

Star Templates for 20" Blocks

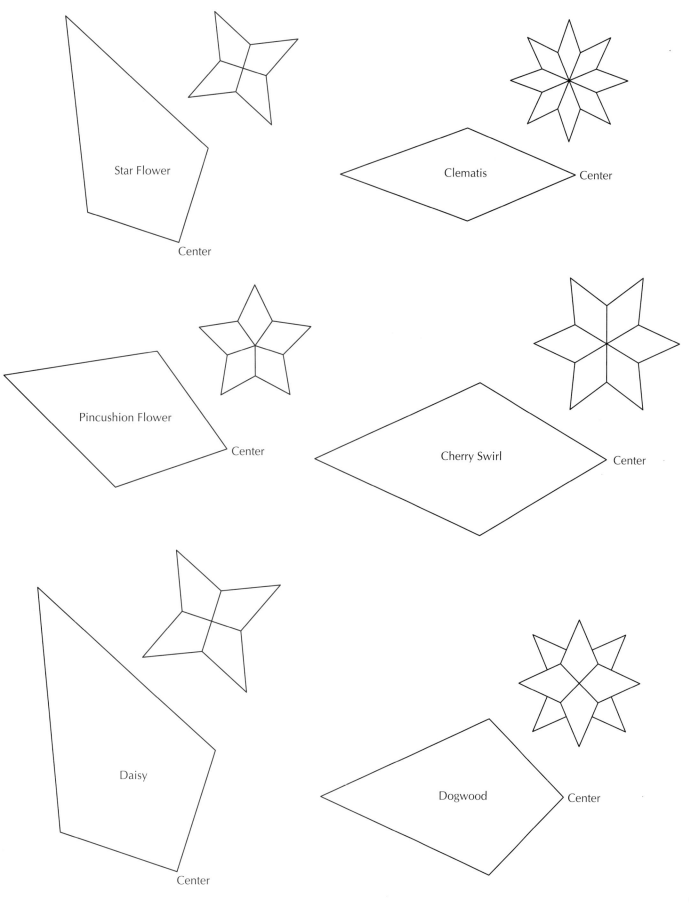

Star Flower

Center

Clematis

Center

Pincushion Flower

Center

Cherry Swirl

Center

Daisy

Center

Dogwood

Center

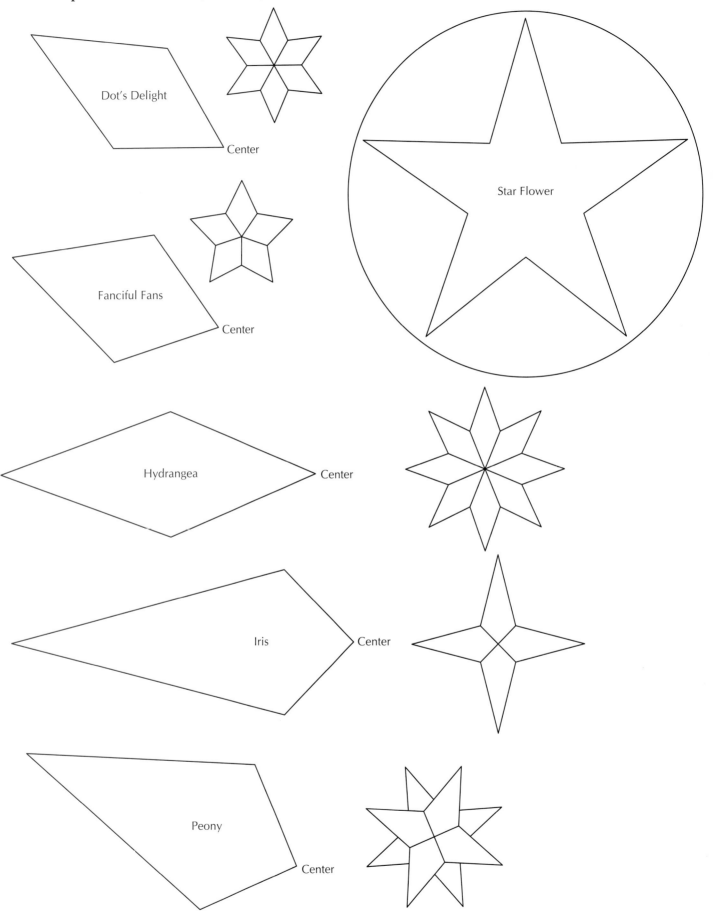

Dot's Delight

Center

Fanciful Fans

Center

Star Flower

Hydrangea

Center

Iris

Center

Peony

Center

7. Stitch all the way around the quilt top, stopping at the folded beginning to the cording fabric. Cut the end of the cording so that it fits snugly into the folded opening; the cording ends should abut.

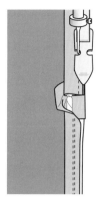

Stop with the needle down.

8. Fold the fabric over the cording ends; finish stitching the cording to the quilt top.

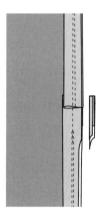

Trim excess fabric.

To finish, layer the quilt top, batting, and backing; then baste. Quilt up to the inner edge of the outer border. Turn the quilt over and trim the batting to the cording seam line. Trim the backing even with the outer raw edge of the quilt top, ¼" beyond the batting edge. Turn the seam allowances of the quilt top and cording over the edge of the batting. Turn under the edges of the quilt backing, baste in place, then sew with an invisible appliqué stitch (see page 12). Finish quilting the outer edges.

If you prefer to use a conventional binding, add it as you normally would, after you finish quilting.

Preparing Your Documentation Patch

Our quilts will likely survive us, so it is important to permanently attach identifying information to each quilt that you make. One way to ensure that the information stays with the quilt is to affix a label to the backing before you quilt the quilt.

Your name should always be on the label. Include the name of the quilt, the date you began and/or finished it, and the fiber content. If you made this quilt for a particular person or occasion, give that information as well. Add photos or pictures to your documentation patch with one of the many photo-transfer products on the market. Make the information as complete as you can.

In addition to the documentation patch, we sign and sometimes date our quilts with a permanent fabric marker on the front in the lower right-hand corner. Always test your pen on a scrap of fabric before writing directly on your quilt. If you have not added a documentation patch, you can write any pertinent information about your quilt directly on the back. Take the time to document your quilt—you will be happy that you did.

Layering the Quilt

Prewash your backing fabric and iron it. The backing fabric should be at least 2" wider, on all sides, than the quilt top. Unless you are using a particularly wide fabric, you will need to piece the backing. When piecing together lengths of fabric, be sure to remove the selvages first, because they will shrink more than the body of the fabric and can distort the quilt.

The batting should be larger than the quilt top by at least 1" on all sides. We prefer 100% cotton batting. There are many new cotton battings on the market that are easier to quilt through than the ones available just a few years ago. Different battings require different amounts of quilting. Read the manufacturer's suggestions for the use of each batting. Select a batting that is suitable for the amount of quilting you intend to put in your quilt. Try different battings, but be sure you like the one you've chosen before using it in a large quilt like this one. Let the batting lie flat for a while to relax it before you layer it into your quilt.

Always add a sleeve to your quilt so it can be hung properly. Prepare the sleeve at the same time you are preparing the quilt backing, especially if you want to make it from the same fabric as the backing. If you piece a backing that is 8½" longer than you need, you can cut off the excess before layering your quilt and make the sleeve from this fabric.

Note from Becky: **You might think you don't need a sleeve on a bed quilt. But I know that I won't always be there to stop someone in the future from nailing my quilt into a wall. I hope that by providing a sleeve, I am giving my quilt a chance.**

It is easier to layer and baste a quilt on a table than it is to baste it on the floor. If you do not have a suitable table, check with your local quilt shop or your church. Often you can find a place with conference tables that you can use. Some quilt shops even have basting frames available for their customers.

1. Lay the backing flat, right side down. Stretching it gently, tape the edges of the backing to the table, to keep it in position.
2. Lay the batting gently over the backing. Some battings have a "clean" side (without cottonseeds) and a "dirty" side (with cottonseeds). Because cottonseeds contain oil that will spot your fabric, make sure the dirty side faces the backing. Do not stretch the batting or you will distort the quilt.
3. Lay the quilt top over the batting, right side up. Be sure to center each layer over the one below. Baste the layers together, using a thread similar in color to the top. Cheap thread in off-colors sometimes leaves color on your quilt. This is not the place to save a few cents.
4. To protect the outer edges of the quilt, fold the excess backing fabric over the batting and outer edges of the quilt top; baste in place.

Finishing the Quilt

Quilt the quilt! We quilt in-the-ditch and around most of the appliqué pieces in each block. Stars in the Garden is machine quilted with rayon thread in colors that match the fabrics. The background behind each block is echo-quilted. The backgrounds would also look good with cross-hatching or stipple quilting. Be creative! Regardless of the quilting pattern, be sure to distribute the quilting evenly across the surface of the quilt. A quilt with heavily quilted and lightly quilted areas will bulge and buckle and will not hang flat.

Our miniature quilt, "Stars in My Little Garden," is hand quilted with 100%-cotton quilting thread. Quilt around all of the appliqué pieces. Refer to the photo on page 26 for ideas on how to quilt the background.

Embellishing the Quilt

Add hard embellishments, such as buttons and beads, after quilting. If you quilt in a frame, these embellishments can be added as you quilt. If you quilt in a hoop or at the machine, it is easier to add them after the quilting is complete. Attach hard embellishments securely. It is important that the stitch you use to attach them goes through all three layers of your quilt. If you use a busy fabric for the back of your quilt, the stitches used to attach these trims will not show.

A variety of buttons accentuate the flower centers. We used one bead in the center of each of the hydrangea blossoms.

> **Tip** Buttons with holes in them, rather than shank buttons, attach more firmly to your quilt. While there are many lovely shank buttons, they have a tendency to flop around on top of the finished quilt, so we use shank buttons sparingly.

Stars in My Little Garden

29½" x 29½"

Choose four of the 8" blocks for your miniature quilt. We chose the Iris, the Dogwood, the Fanciful Fan, and the Star Flower. Please read all previous instructions to complete the blocks.

Fabric Requirements and Cutting

Block Backgrounds: ⅓ yd.
Cut four 10" squares for the block backgrounds.

Inner Border: ⅛ yd.
Cut 2 strips, each 1½" x 16½", for the top and bottom of the blocks.
Cut 2 strips, each 1½" x 18½", for the sides of the blocks.

Pieced Corner Triangles: a variety of small pieces of fabric, totaling about 1¼ yds. Cut 32 strips, each 4½" x 10½", for the pieced triangles.

Outer Border: ⅓ yd.
Cut 2 strips, each 2½" x 26", for the top and bottom of the quilt.
Cut 2 strips, each 2½" x 29½", for the sides of the quilt.

Backing and Sleeve: 1⅓ yds.
Cut a 34" x 34" square for the backing.
Cut an 8½" x 29½" strip for the sleeve.

Trimming the Blocks

After your appliqué is complete, press the blocks. Always press your blocks wrong side up. Trim the pressed appliqué blocks to 8½" square. Sew them together.

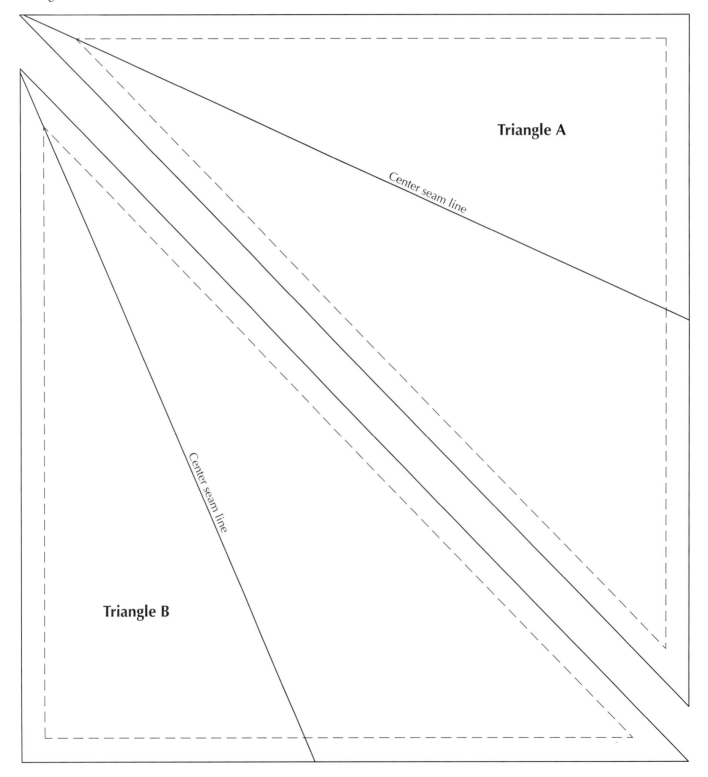

Triangle A

Center seam line

Center seam line

Triangle B

Constructing the Pieced
Corner Triangles

Each corner of this miniature quilt is made up of two triangles A and two triangles B as shown below. There are eight strips of fabric in each pieced corner triangle. Choose the fabrics for your quilt corners and fan them out on your design wall. Audition these fabrics with your completed blocks. We waited to choose these fabrics until our four blocks were complete and sewn together. Then we chose the inner border and the fabrics for the pieced corner triangles. It is important to find just the right fabrics to complement your blocks without overpowering them.

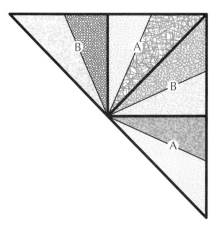

1. Make a clear plastic template of triangle A and triangle B on page 40. Mark the center seam line on your templates.
2. Once you have chosen the fabrics, cut them as directed on page 39. Refer to the pieced corner triangle illustration above. Sew the fabrics together into pairs. Lay the proper template over each pair of fabrics and cut out 8 of triangle A and 8 of triangle B.

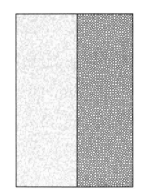

Sew the strips for the pieced corner triangles together into pairs. Be aware of their placement as you sew. You might want to put the sewn pairs back in order on your design wall.

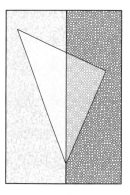

Lay the proper template over one of the stitched pairs. Align the center seam line marked on your template with the center seam line of the fabric. Make sure that the template is lined up so the fabrics you have chosen are in the right place.

3. Arrange and sew the A and B triangles into pairs. Join the pairs into a large triangle.

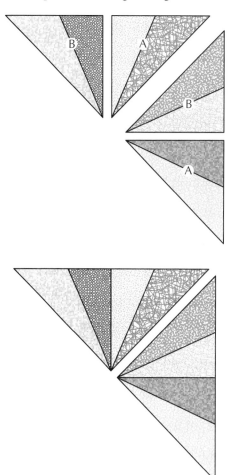

Finishing the Quilt

Attach the outer borders to your miniature quilt. Add cording or prepare traditional binding to attach after quilting. Make your documentation patch and appliqué it to the backing fabric. Layer, baste, and quilt your quilt. Finish the outer edges of your quilt. Attach the sleeve to the back. (Refer to pages 33–38 to finish your miniature quilt.)

About the Authors

Linda Jenkins and Becky Goldsmith met at a gathering of the Green Country Quilter's Guild in Tulsa, Oklahoma, in 1986. Both were active in the guild, and over the years they became good friends. Together, they started Piece O' Cake Designs in 1994. That same year, Linda and her husband, Paul, moved to Pagosa Springs, Colorado, and Becky, her husband, Steve, and their two boys moved to Sherman, Texas. Living in this age of technology made the distance between them manageable, and their business has prospered.

Linda, who owned and managed a beauty salon for many years before she started quilting, has a fine eye for color that developed through years as a hair colorist and makeup artist. Becky's background in art and interior design enabled her to take the ideas in their minds and put them on paper.

Both Linda and Becky teach and lecture. Becky has had quilts hanging in a number of shows nationally and has won numerous awards. *Stars in the Garden* is their second book for That Patchwork Place; *Welcome to the North Pole* was published in 1997.

Linda and Becky

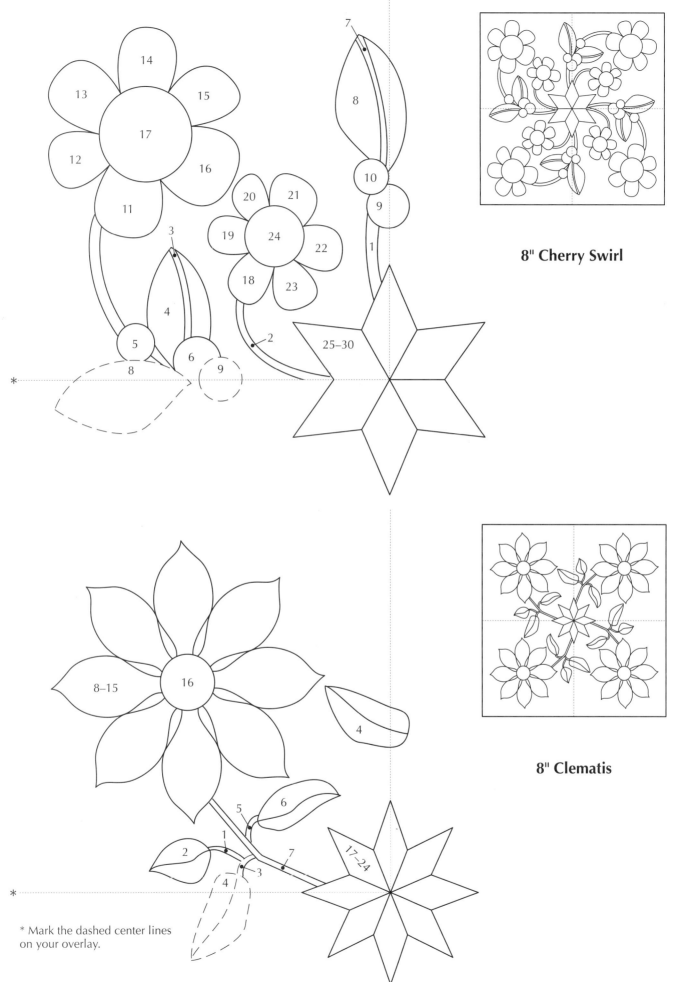

8" Cherry Swirl

8" Clematis

* Mark the dashed center lines on your overlay.

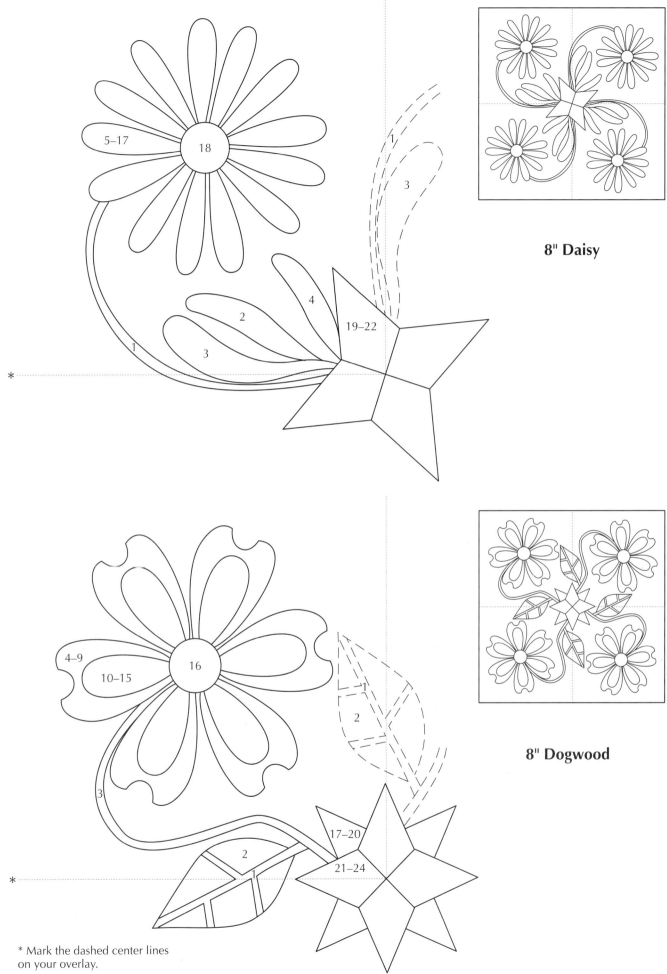

8" Daisy

8" Dogwood

* Mark the dashed center lines
on your overlay.

44

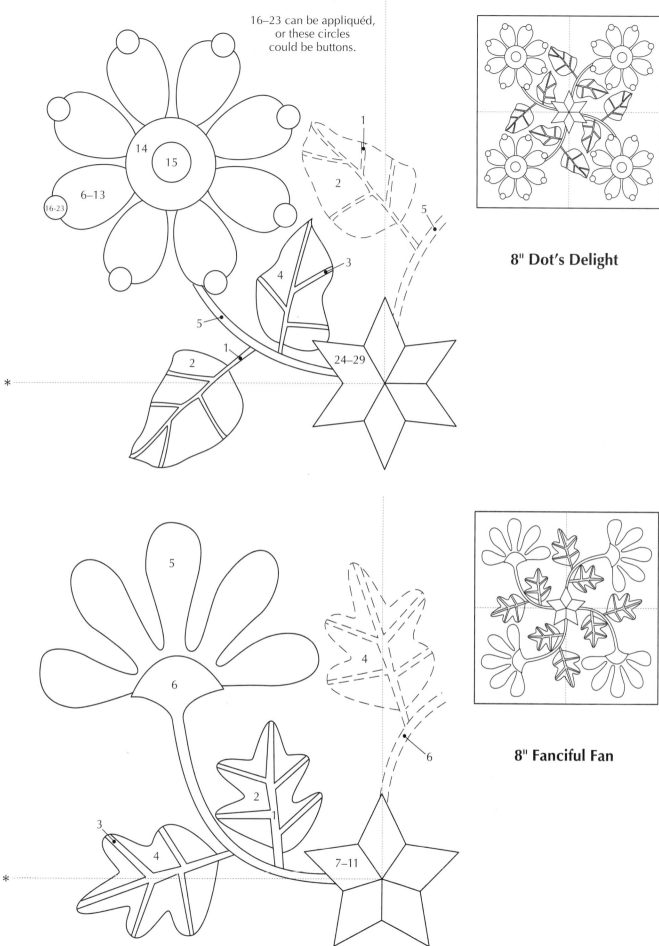

16–23 can be appliquéd, or these circles could be buttons.

14

15

6–13

16-23

1

2

5

4

3

5

1

2

24–29

8" Dot's Delight

* Mark the dashed center lines on your overlay.

5

6

4

6

2

1

3

4

7–11

8" Fanciful Fan

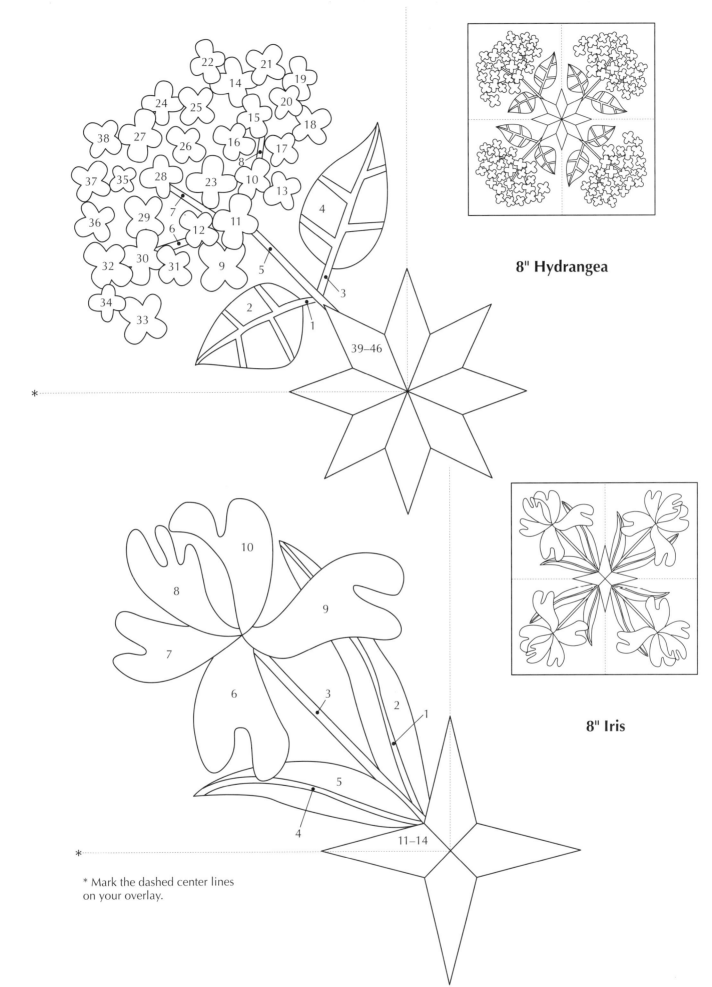

8" Hydrangea

8" Iris

* Mark the dashed center lines
on your overlay.

46

#6 is one large, rounded piece.

6 9
8
12 10
13
7 11
5

1
2
3 4

14–17
18–21

1
2
3
4
5

8" Peony

14
6–13
16 15

#14 is one piece, a circle with scalloped edges.

5
1
2
4 3

17–21

8" Pincushion Flower

* Mark the dashed center lines on your overlay.

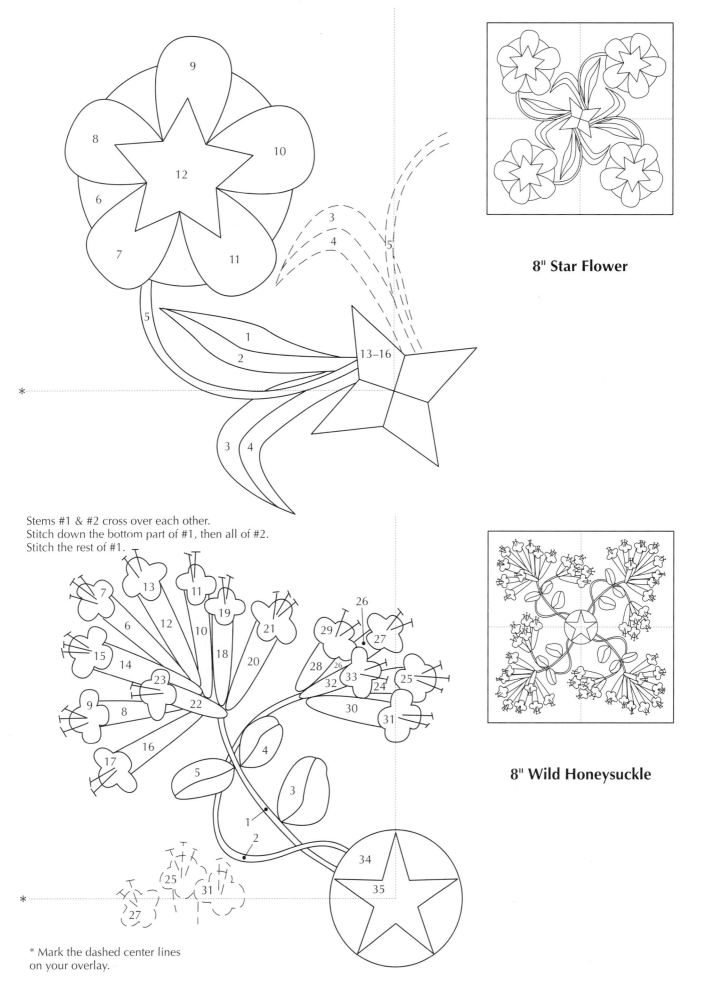

8" Star Flower

Stems #1 & #2 cross over each other.
Stitch down the bottom part of #1, then all of #2.
Stitch the rest of #1.

8" Wild Honeysuckle

* Mark the dashed center lines
on your overlay.